IMAGES
of America

EUCLID BEACH PARK

IMAGES
of America

EUCLID BEACH PARK

Euclid Beach Park Now

ARCADIA
PUBLISHING

Published by Arcadia Publishing
Charleston, South Carolina

Library of Congress Control Number: 2012943732

For all general information, please contact Arcadia Publishing:
Telephone 843-853-2070
Fax 843-853-0044
E-mail sales@arcadiapublishing.com
For customer service and orders:
Toll-Free 1-888-313-2665

Visit us on the Internet at www.arcadiapublishing.com

*To all those with fond memories of Euclid Beach
Park . . . yesterday, today, and forever*

CONTENTS

Acknowledgments   6

Introduction   7

1.   The Early Years   11

2.   A Walk through the Park   35

3.   The Memories Live On   113

ACKNOWLEDGMENTS

Our group was founded in 1989 and originally named Euclid Beach Park Nuts. In the mid-2000s, the name was changed to Euclid Beach Park Now. Our mission from the onset has been to support the historical education of Euclid Beach Park through lectures, displays, exhibits, and memorabilia shows, as well as television and radio appearances and any other available media. We also support the preservation of physical items and memorabilia from Euclid Beach Park owned by other organizations, private individuals, or any other entity.

We would like to thank Arcadia Publishing for affording us the opportunity to create this work and, in so doing, supporting our mission statement. This project would not be possible without the support and assistance of the entire Euclid Beach Park Now Board of Directors. The board's collective knowledge of the park proved to be invaluable. Many of the members attended writing sessions, proofread copy, and performed research. Listed in alphabetical order, the board consists of Beverly Ericsson, Oscar Ericsson, John Frato (president), Kathleen Frato, Howard Kast, Janice Kast, William Kless, Wendell Kucera, Rosemarie Kusold (treasurer), Robert MacCallum, John Marn, Dave Masek, Fletcher Milan, Rudy Nagode, Jay Rightnour, Jim Seman (secretary), Kathy Seman, Lorna Vaughns, Sandra Wesley, Kathy Wickens, and Richard Wickens (vice president). The core writing team of John Frato, Rosemarie Kusold, and Jim Seman deserve special thanks for their long hours of work and diligence to detail. William Kless is responsible for the photograph selection and also the layout of the first two chapters. He spent countless hours preparing images for use in the book. He was assisted by John Marn, who not only compiled the images for the last chapter but also attended numerous writing sessions. A non-board member also played a significant role in the book's creation: Lee O. Bush, who coauthored both *Euclid Beach Park Is Closed for the Season* and *Euclid Beach Park a Second Look*, provided invaluable advice and support as well as text that appears throughout the book.

During the research for this publication, it quickly became apparent that some of the same images were present in various photograph collections. With Euclid Beach being so popular, many photographs were copied repeatedly. The vast majority of images selected for this work come from three sources:

• The Cleveland State University, Michael Schwartz Library, Special Collection, which included photographs from the Bruce Young Collection, the Humphrey Family Collection, Parade Studios, the *Cleveland Plain Dealer*, and the Brookins Collection/ Harry Christiansen.
• The Euclid Beach Boys Collection owned by Joe Tomaro and John Frato, which includes photographs from the Edward C. Chukayne Collection, Jerry Keck collection, and Bill Parker collection.
• A combined photograph collection owned by Jim Seman and Jim Wise.

The balance of the images, in no particular order, are from Jon Blakemore, Lee O. Bush, Goodyear Tire & Rubber Company records (Archival Services, the University of Akron, Akron Ohio), Lorna Vaughns (Holtz collection), Howard Kast, Douglas Keener, William Kless, Wendell Kucera, Robert N. MacCallum, John Marn, Fletcher Milan, Dudley H. Scott (Scott family collection), Richard Reese, Chuck Russell, Richard Wickens, *Sun News*, Sylvia Cutshall Ferrara Zampino, Euclid Beach Park Now Archives (Rose Marie Thomas collection), and Richard Fleischman + Partners Architects.

For those of who submitted images not chosen, we thank you for your support. We were blessed with a tremendous amount of photographs to choose from, however space was limited.

INTRODUCTION

With the Industrial Revolution came the migration of people from rural areas to cities. With this population shift, people had more free time and disposable income for entertainment. New York City's Coney Island became a popular entertainment venue at the end of this era and was influential in the development of amusement parks in other cities—they began popping up everywhere. A picnic grove would build a ride, usually a merry-go-round, Ferris wheel, or roller coaster, and then continue to add other rides, attractions, and concessions in subsequent years. Some amusement parks, first known as trolley parks, were started by streetcar companies, usually at the end of a line to generate weekend business. Cleveland had many minor parks operating in the 1890s, but none of them stood out.

On October 23, 1894, five businessmen from Cleveland incorporated the Euclid Beach Park Company. In 1895, the company secured an option on 63.06 acres of land on Lake Erie's southern shore in Euclid Township. After making improvements to the parcel, Euclid Beach Park opened on Saturday, June 22, 1895. The structures built for the opening included a wooden Pier, a Dance Pavilion with an 18,000-square-foot red maple floor, a Bath House with an upper-level restaurant, and the Avenue Theatre, which was used for live theater and vaudeville shows. By 1897, a number of new attractions were installed, including a walk-through fun house called the Crystal Maze, the Ferris Wheel, the Switchback Railway, and the Merry-Go-Round. As crowds grew larger, more improvements were made to the park. Many local businessmen chose the grounds of Euclid Beach to hold their annual company picnics.

The Humphrey family operated very successful popcorn stands in the Cleveland area and had a storefront site in the center of the city at the southwest corner of Ontario Street and Public Square, which they opened in 1895. The Humphrey family also opened a popcorn stand at the park in 1896. They viewed the atmosphere at Euclid Beach Park to be unsavory, as the park had a beer garden, sideshows, and gambling. They suggested to park management to eliminate these features, but they refused. In 1899, the Humphreys chose not to renew their lease because they were uncomfortable working where drinking, gambling, and questionable sideshows were condoned. The opening of Manhattan Beach at East 140th Street in 1900 added to the financial challenges the park owners already faced, and they made the decision to close Euclid Beach.

Upon hearing the news of the closure, the Humphreys offered to lease the park from the owners. Their plan was to operate it in accordance with their New England high moral values. The deal was made, and in the spring of 1901 the park opened without the beer garden, fakers, gamblers, and sideshows. A free gate became the order of the day. Naysayers felt the Humphreys were doomed to failure, but the new family atmosphere was successful. Under their ownership and management, the lakefront amusement park was operated on the foundation of fair dealing, clean entertainment, and pleasant surroundings. An early slogan for the park was "Nothing to Depress or Demoralize."

The Humphreys added rides and attractions each year. Between 1901 and 1910, new amusements included the Velvet Coaster (later renamed the Aero Dips), Figure 8 Coaster, Aerial Swing, Scenic Railway, World Theatre, Flying Ponies, Log Cabin, and a grand four-row Carousel, built by the Philadelphia Toboggan Company. The Derby Racer (later renamed the Racing Coaster) was a significant addition, which remained a fixture at Euclid Beach for decades after its construction in 1913. It was designed by John Miller and consisted of two trains that raced each other on a continuous, parallel track.

The park changed significantly during the 1920s and 1930s. Two signature roller coasters were designed and built during this time that would be synonymous with Euclid Beach until closing day. The Thriller was built over the winter of 1923 and was ready for opening day in 1924. Built by the Philadelphia Toboggan Company at an estimated cost of $90,000, the ride paid for itself before the end of its first season. The last high ride constructed was the Flying Turns. A chain lift pulled the three-car train up the first hill, and then the cars freewheeled to the end of the ride in an open-top, wood-lined barrel. The ride was designed to simulate a bobsled, and the close quarters gave riders the mistaken impression they were traveling at much higher speeds. Other rides added during this building boom included the Great American Racing Derby, Sleepy Hollow Railroad, Flying Scooters, Laff in the Dark, Mill Chute (later redesigned and renamed Over the Falls), Red Bug Boulevard, Surprise House with Laughing Sam and Laughing Sal, Dodgems, Dippy Whip, Bug, Bubble Bounce, and Colonnade, with Kiddie Land located at its southern end. Additionally, the wicker gondolas on the Aerial Swing were replaced with Aeroplanes and later the Buck Roger–style stainless steel Rocket Ships designed and built by the park's maintenance staff. Also notable during this time was the death of Dudley S. Humphrey II on September 19, 1933. He was the family patriarch and Humphrey Company president from opening day in 1901. By the time of his death, the vast majority of the park's signature rides were already installed.

After World War II, interest in amusement parks diminished, and many turn-of-the-century parks closed. Euclid Beach Park struggled and attempted to increase attendance with new attractions. During the 1950s and 1960s, major additions included the Rotor, Turnpike, Swinging Gyms, Giant Slide, Coffee Break, and the Antique Cars (placed in the Roller Rink building after it was no longer used for skating). The Great American Racing Derby was sold to Cedar Point, possibly as a means to raise revenue. In its place, the Ferris Wheel and Tilt-a-Whirl were installed. Euclid Beach Park, like many amusement parks across the United States, hosted rock-and-roll concerts. The hope was to introduce a new generation to the park and hopefully obtain loyal repeat park guests. Euclid Beach Park hosted the Lovin' Spoonful, Gary Lewis and the Playboys, and The Beach Boys to name a few. In their recording "Amusement Parks U.S.A.," The Beach Boys pay tribute to Euclid Beach Park with the line, "At Euclid Beach on the Flying Turns, I bet you can't keep from smilin'."

The Humphreys announced at the end of the 1968 season that the park would close the following year. Euclid Beach Park closed on September 28, 1969. Competition had increased sharply from Cedar Point and Geauga Lake. Euclid Beach had lost its picnic base: communities and companies that usually held yearly outings at the beach were now booking their picnics elsewhere. The park was landlocked, with no room for expansion. The Humphreys could have expanded into the neighboring trailer park but chose not to; they did not want to uproot the residents, and closing the trailer park would have eliminated their only source of profits for some of the last years.

Euclid Beach was the most beloved of Cleveland's amusement parks. The operating policies of the Humphrey Company attracted many families, as well as community, church, school, lodge, and company outings. Euclid Beach saw its competitors open and close, outlasting them all until it ceased operations on September 28, 1969. A reporter who interviewed D.S. Humphrey in August 1930's *Amusement Park Management* article "From Tickets—Not Money" best summarized the popularity of the park:

> There are certain shrewd subtleties about the management and the policies of Euclid Beach Park which present themselves to your attention only after you have attentively studied this fine resort. Perhaps the quickest way to discover these subtleties is by comparison with other parks. The Humphrey management has shaped Euclid Beach Park to fit exactly the tastes and desires of the largest number of patrons that could be expected to come to it. Therefore Euclid Beach Park, although it is a big park and a clean one and a refined one, has no "high hat" atmosphere—and no "low hat" attraction either. The Humphrey management has accomplished the happy medium. It is not managed to attract particularly the higher class of patron that is seen at Rye's Playland, for instance, nor the more numerous type that mass into Coney Island, New York. It has managed to attract everybody and to make them feel at home. Not too many decorations, not too much landscaping, no buildings

that look as if it might cost a lot of money to go into them—just plain but substantial and satisfying amusement fare that gives dime for dime value. It might not go in some locations but there is no doubt it being a success at Euclid Beach. "Perhaps," as Mr. Humphrey remarked to the writer, "we don't know how to run a park—but here it is." The subject of money is kept submerged as much as possible at this park. Nowhere, from the beginning to the end of a visit there, is it compulsory to spend money. No one asks you to, yells at you, no one urges you to spend a dime. In fact, it is possible to spend an entire and happy day at the park without giving up one cent. "Tickets—Not Money," is one of the slogans of the park. Every cent that comes from a patron, with the exception of the cafeteria and two small stands, goes into the universal ticket booths. There the patron receives strips of tickets good for five cents each—as many or as few as he wishes to buy. It is easier to comprehend the extent to which this "Tickets—Not Money" slogan has been carried in Euclid Beach Park when you realize that even refreshments and soft drink stands accept tickets only. Loganberry required two tickets, ginger ale for one ticket, etc.

There are no barkers. No spielers invite you to step in or take a ride. No frankfurter man informs you that they are "red hot." It isn't necessary, somehow, in Euclid Beach Park. You sense that everything is as it should be before you've been in the park five minutes.

The people of Cleveland trust the Humphreys and they trust Euclid Beach Park. They are a Cleveland institution. There seems to be no doubt in anybody's mind—whether or not he is a patron—that, what the Humphreys say and do is all right. No one thinks of mistrusting a ride or refreshment. Let us take the loganberry juice stand, for instance. A sign above the counter tells us that the juice is shipped directly to the park from the west coast, the home of loganberries. And you can believe this writer when he says that this loganberry drink at Euclid Beach is one of the best, if not the best drink sold in any amusement park. Even the creamy whip at Euclid Beach is something more than sweetened bubbles—it is as satisfying as a dish of ice cream. And the candy—that is made right before your eyes with real butter, and real cream and sugar. It is no wonder the people of Cleveland trust the Humphreys. And a good many of them know Dudley S. Humphrey personally. They know him by sight and do not hesitate to speak to him when they see him. And the children—most all of them can recognize that electric wheel chair of his a mile off—flock around him.

It is our hope that the images we selected will transport readers back to the days when Euclid Beach was open for the season. Those lucky enough to have visited the park can relive fond memories. For anyone who never felt the cool lake breeze while riding the Rocket Ships or unconsciously began to laugh in front of Sal in the Surprise House, perhaps those readers will begin to understand why Euclid Beach was such a special, magical place.

One

THE EARLY YEARS

The main entrance to Euclid Beach Park was located on Lake Shore Boulevard a short distance from East 156th Street. The original Arch was constructed of wood. By the late 1920s, it was decided to cover it with permastone, a product that looks very much like real stone. The men directing traffic were members of the Euclid Beach Police force.

The first entrance to Euclid Beach Park is pictured here. The park opened on Saturday, June 22, 1895, on approximately 63 acres of land. It was located on the shores of Lake Erie, eight miles east of Cleveland's Public Square. The Dance Pavilion, Theatre, Pier, and Bath House were constructed for the first season. No rides were installed until the second season.

In 1904, Dudley S. Humphrey II made a deal with the Cleveland Traction Company (which owned and operated trolleys) that the trolleys would run into Euclid Beach Park and discharge passengers at a station within the park. In later years, this station would become the popcorn and candy-kiss stand. The trolley station would remain in this location until 1907 when it was moved to another location inside the park. Then, in 1924, it was moved to the Lake Shore Boulevard location.

An early view of the grand entranceway to the park faces the lake towards the Dance Pavilion and the Aerial Swing. The Pier was a fixture at Euclid Beach from opening day in 1895. It was originally divided down the center by a wooden railing to separate arriving and departing steamer passengers.

During the first five years of operation, the canopied area at the end of the Pier is where the majority of visitors arrived onboard one of the two steamers, also known as the "Tubs," owned by the Euclid Beach Park Company. The *Duluth* and the *Superior* steamers were painted white with bright red letters and could each carry 800 passengers from downtown Cleveland. This view looks north from the beach with two lifeguards in the foreground.

An early version of the Bath House featured a partially open second floor. In 1909, the second floor was enclosed, and a series of restaurants occupied this space throughout the years. One of the most popular eateries, Crosby's-on-the-Lake, opened in 1931.

Bathing attire was very conservative for both men and women, and there were strict rules governing swimwear. In most cases, costumes were made of wool.

The Bath House was one of the first buildings at the park; it was constructed for the 1895 opening. On the lower level, swimmers could rent lockers, towels, and swimsuits. Bathers were given a metal tag with a locker number to pin to their suits until they returned.

These early aviators standing next to a biplane are, from left to right, Eugene Ely, James "Bud" Mars, and Glenn H. Curtiss. On August 31, 1910, Curtiss took off from the beach at Euclid Beach Park and flew to Cedar Point in Sandusky, Ohio. At the time, it was the longest flight over water. The next day, he took off from the beach at Cedar Point for the return flight to Euclid Beach Park.

A rectangular pool was located east of the Bath House. The pool had strict regulations on bathing attire: a bathing garment had to be long enough to cover the limbs and high enough to cover the chest, with no gaudy colors. Patrons could swim in the pool or the lake, as the activity was very popular in the 1920s. The pool was removed in the late 1920s due to winter storm damage.

The Sea Swing, pictured here in 1920, occupied the circular pool just west of the Bath House on the beach next to the Pier. A sort-of water ride, with a merry-go-round configuration but without horses, it whisked riders in strap-like seats just above the water's surface. The rotation was powered electrically. The Fountain was placed in this area once the ride was dismantled.

The Log Cabin was originally built for the 1901 Pan American Exposition held in Buffalo, New York; it served as the Forestry Building. The structure was purchased by the Humphrey Company, disassembled in 1902, loaded onto barges, and floated west on Lake Erie to Euclid Beach Park, where it was reassembled. It was the first structure seen to the left when entering the park from the main parking lot. It served as headquarters for company and community picnics and as a dance hall. The oval windows shown in the photograph were later replaced with conventional rectangular windows.

Park employees pictured here are boarding a streetcar at Euclid Beach with money sacks filled with $20,000 in cash receipts from their Fourth of July business. This publicity stunt was arranged by the Humphreys not only to highlight the park's popularity but more importantly spotlight the trolleys as a safe and inexpensive way to travel to and from the park.

The Roller Rink was built in 1904. It was a large, 230-foot-long building, and the skating path was 35 feet wide. In the center were two enclosed areas: one in front of the Gavioli Band Organ, for experienced skaters, and the other behind the organ for beginners. Wooden window panels were open to admit the cool lake breezes as needed.

The Gavioli Band Organ was originally purchased for use at the Humphreys' ice-skating rink, The Elysium, and relocated to the Roller Rink at Euclid Beach. It remained at that location even after the Roller Rink was closed and transformed into the Antique Car ride. It was sold to a doctor in New England and then went to a collector in Chicago, where it remains.

The Dance Pavilion was one of the original 1895 structures, enduring until the park closed in 1969. A grand dance floor, measuring 18,000 square feet and made of red maple, could accommodate 1,000 couples at one time. Not only were dancers attracted to the Dance Pavilion, but also many park guests would view the whirling and rush of hundreds of dancers from the balcony (at no charge). Over the years, some changes were made, one of which was the addition of two mirrored balls hung from the ceiling near each end of the room. During slow dances, colored spotlights bounced off the balls, which filled the room with countless dots of colored lights.

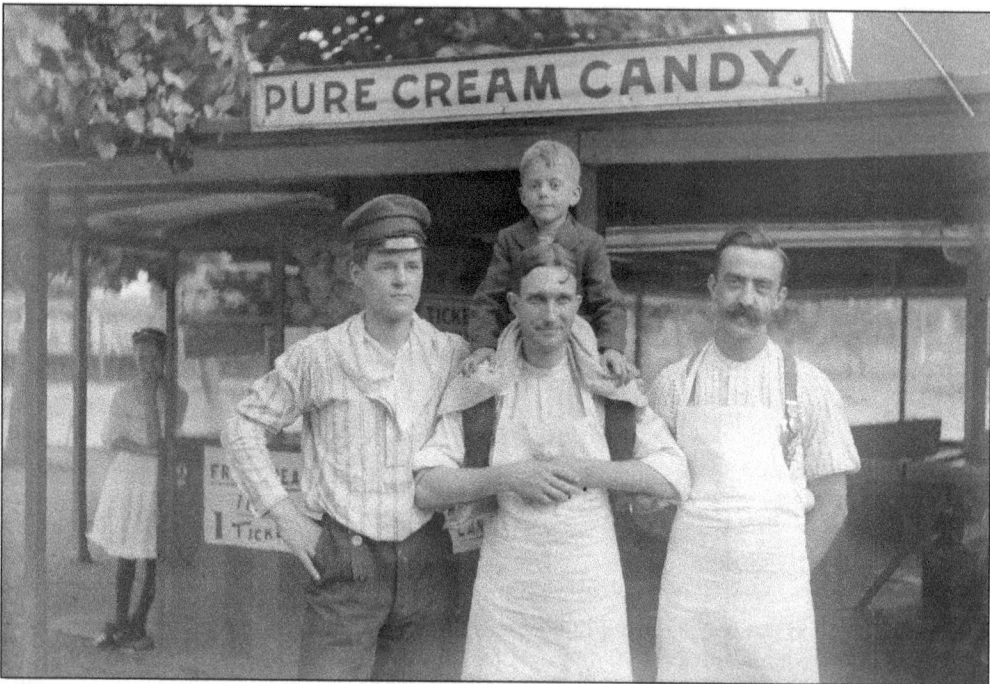

The gentleman with the hat is Harvey Humphrey, and the girl in the background, leaning against the stand, is Harvey's sister Louise. Harvey and Louise were the son and daughter of Dudley S. Humphrey II and his wife, Effie. They pose near an early concession stand that featured pure cream candy, later called candy kisses, with two park employees and an unidentified boy.

One of the favorite cold drinks at the park was Phez Loganberry Juice, which was sold at the stand on the right. It outsold Hire's Root Beer and Vernor's ginger ale; however, the stand operators found that the juice drink, when not refrigerated long enough, would ferment into alcohol. When the Humphrey family found out, this was the end of loganberry juice at Euclid Beach Park.

In the early 1910s, patrons could buy an ice-cream sandwich, a dish of ice cream, a milk shake, sandwich, piece of pie, or soda from this stand. A glass ticket box is on the right side of the counter. Money was not exchanged; tickets were used to purchase the confections.

The Shooting Gallery, pictured here, was located in the Colonnade, and the rifles used real bullets. It was one of the few games of skill in the park. Prizes were not awarded, and patrons merely competed against one another. Fifteen shots could be purchased with two tickets.

The World Theatre was constructed in 1902 and used for the sole purpose of showing the relatively new moving pictures. It remained at the park until 1920, at which time it was razed to make room for the Dodgem and the Laff in the Dark.

The Avenue Theatre was built in 1895 and used for stage productions, vaudeville, and special events. The backstage area of the building at the west end was converted into the Annex after theatrical productions ceased and was used as a picnic headquarters.

This photograph shows the Poland family camping at Euclid Beach's "Tent City." For this family, the Humphrey incentive plan included moving the entire family to Cleveland, making a loan to the father to open a tailor shop, providing work for all the children who wanted jobs at Euclid Beach Park, and providing housing for the family in Tent City in the summer and in the employee housing development during the winter months.

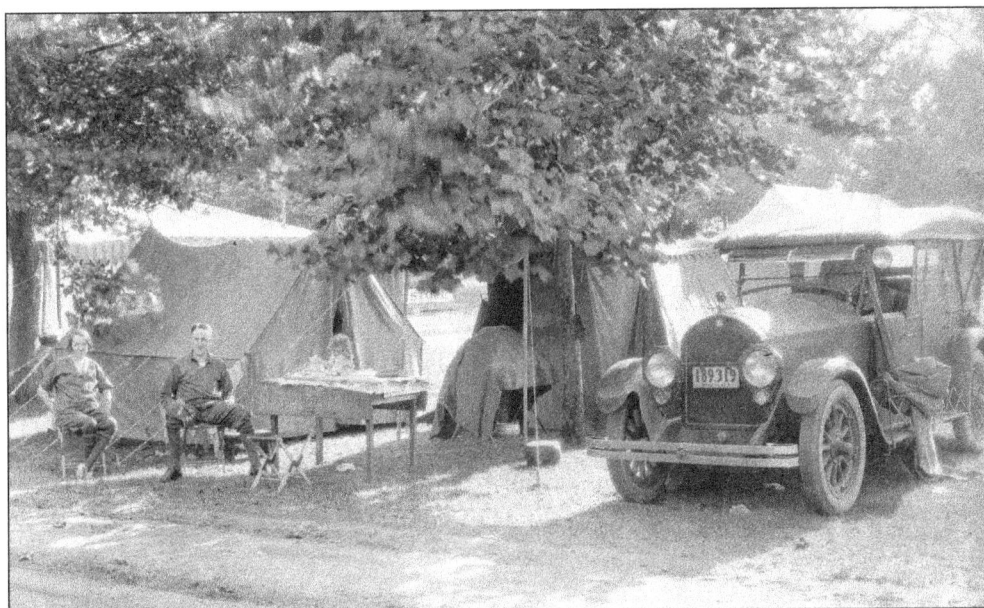

The campgrounds were popular with those who did not live close enough to make a day trip to Euclid Beach and allowed them to visit the park economically. In 1923, this family in Tent City shows how close to the tent their car was parked. Today, the campground is a mobile-home park.

Euclid Beach Park patrons are pictured sitting in an early bus used for sightseeing in the park and the adjoining campgrounds. The bus was manufactured by the White Motor Company of Cleveland, Ohio, and was replaced in later years by the Auto Train.

The first Sleepy Hollow Train was a steam engine installed near the Scenic Railway in the early 1900s, but it was removed after only a few years due to park expansion. The second steam engine was purchased in 1926 and installed outside of Kiddieland. The Humphreys' concern for safety resulted in the park's chief engineer converting the power unit from steam to compressed air.

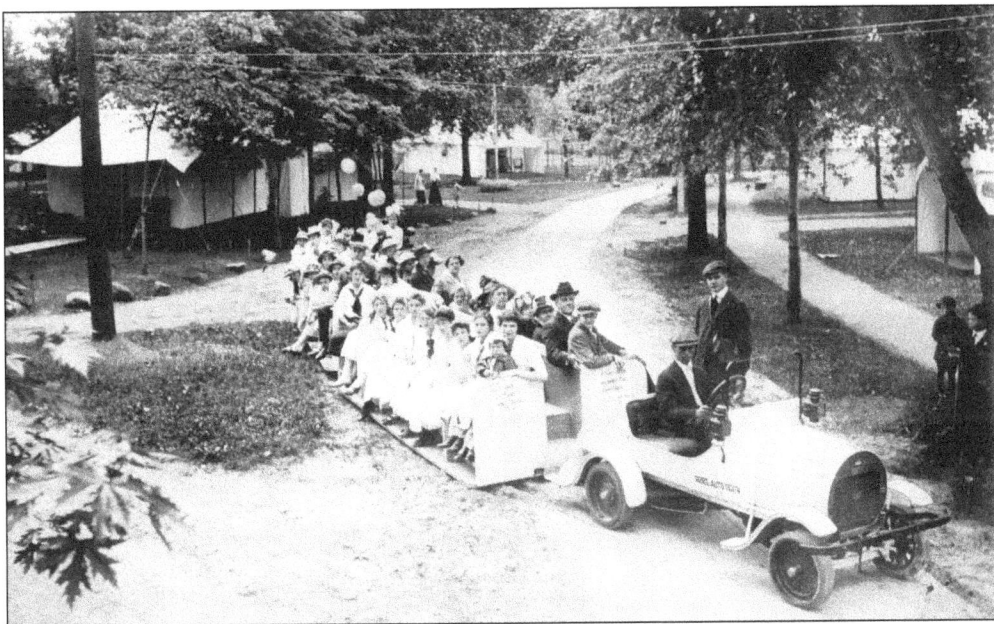

The Auto Train consisted of a gas-powered tractor vehicle that pulled three cars. This was more of an excursion than a ride. It came to the park in 1916 from the San Francisco Pan American Expo. It would pick up passengers on the park's Midway and carried them through the park and the campgrounds. It was a slow, leisurely way to see all sides of the park. This ride was staffed by two employees: one to take tickets and one to drive. When the park closed, it went to the community of Mayfield Village, Ohio, and now part of the ride is owned by Western Reserve Historical Society.

The first Ferris Wheel at Euclid Beach Park was built by the Buckeye Observation Wheel Company. It was installed for the park's second season in 1896 and then removed in 1902 when construction of the Roller Rink began.

The Flying Ponies was made by the Herschell-Spillman Carousel Company in 1903. Unlike other carousels, the horses did not move up and down but were suspended from above and allowed to swing freely. The platform was slanted at a 10-degree angle. As the machine turned, the horses would swing inward at the high point and outward at the low point. The machine was removed after the 1934 season.

Euclid Beach Park's first Merry-Go-Round was installed for the second season of operation in 1896. It was a track machine; the motion of the ride's figures was activated from underneath its platform. The Merry-Go-Round was manufactured by Armitage Herschell Company of North Tonawanda, New York.

The Euclid Beach Grand Carousel was manufactured and installed by the Philadelphia Toboggan Company for the 1910 season. The machine consisted of 58 hand-carved wooden horses and two chariots. The ride operator would ring a bell to signal the start and end of the ride. The Carousel continued to provide enjoyment to riders through the 1969 season. It was sold to Palace Playland in Old Orchard Beach, Maine, where it operated until 1996. It was then sold at auction in Cleveland and donated to the Western Reserve Historical Society.

The Humphreys, who had a lifelong fascination with aviation, installed the Aerial Swing at the park in 1902. Passengers boarded on ground level into wicker gondolas, which were designed to resemble those found under airships. The Humphreys strengthened the tower in the early years, which allowed for the installation of heavier ride vehicles.

The nation became obsessed with aviation after Charles Lindberg's flight in 1927. The Humphreys engaged the Traver Engineering Company of Beaver Falls, Pennsylvania, to design and install cars that resembled biplanes. The ride was renamed the Aeroplanes, and the loading platform was raised 15 feet above ground level.

The Switchback Railway was the park's first roller coaster. LaMarcus Adna Thompson, who was considered the "father of roller coasters," designed it. The ride operators would push the train out of the loading platform down the first hill. The ride relied on gravity to reach the other end, where it was manually switched over for the trip back to the starting platform. The ride was dismantled and removed from the park in 1903, replaced by the Figure 8 roller coaster for the 1904 season.

The Red Bug Boulevard Cars were powered by electric motors that were supplied with current from storage batteries inside the vehicles. Originally, they did not have the front bonnet covers (as pictured). The Humphreys felt that ladies attired in either skirts or dresses were unladylike when they rode in the cars. The covers were designed and installed by the park maintenance shop. This ride offered the thrill of racing, much like the go-kart tracks of today. It was removed in the 1930s.

The Figure 8 roller coaster was installed in 1904 in the area where the Switchback Railway was located. It was a gravity ride, manufactured by the Philadelphia Toboggan Company. It had a figure-eight layout and featured a circular loading platform. It had modest speed but was a popular ride. Riders sat in a single car that held four people.

A wooden walkway ran from the Dance Pavilion to the loading station of the Figure 8 ride. In 1908, this roller coaster was razed, and the Velvet Coaster was built in its place for the 1909 season. The Figure 8 was a popular ride in the early part of the century and was constructed at many other amusement parks. Today, only one remains in existence.

The Scenic Railway was built at Euclid Beach Park in 1907. The rather ornate building, for Humphrey standards, was quite the eye-catcher. A train of riders is on the second level, moving to the loading platform.

There were two Whips that operated at Euclid Beach Park. The second ride was installed in the Avenue Theatre location in 1938 and was named the Dippy Whip. The Whip pictured here was installed around 1915, just west of the tall, ornate tower of the Scenic Railway's loading platform. Both the outdoor and indoor Whips were manufactured by the William F. Mangels Company.

The Scenic Railway operated from 1907 through 1937. LaMarcus Thompson Scenic Railways were popular at many amusement parks worldwide. This form of roller coaster was based on the ride's earliest design, with flanged wheels like railroad cars. It preceded the under-friction, safety-wheel configuration invented by John Miller in 1913. It functioned in much the same way as San Francisco cable cars. Two men on each train operated a lever that would grasp a cable between the tracks and pull the car up the hill; there were several cables throughout the track layout. The speed was determined by the brakeman on each train.

At the end of the souvenir stand, one could buy a helium balloon with two park tickets. In later years, the helium tanks were disguised to look like clowns. The helium was dispensed from the clown's mouth to the delight of children.

The Custer Kiddie Cars was one of the earliest kiddie rides at the park. It was located along the walkway from the streetcar stop near the future site of the Colonnade. It was replaced by the Pony Track, which featured live horses.

The early Midway is visible here, with the boarded pathway in front of the Grand Carousel, which was manufactured by the Philadelphia Toboggan Company. A ticket booth is visible in front of the Carousel enclosure. A concession stand at the lower right of the photograph featured Wilbur's Sweet Chocolate, pepsin gum, and a penny scale to check one's weight.

On the bluff above the Pier, the Auto Train makes a scenic trip through the park. During this busy day, a crowd has gathered on the Pier to enjoy the cool lake breeze.

Two

A WALK
THROUGH THE PARK

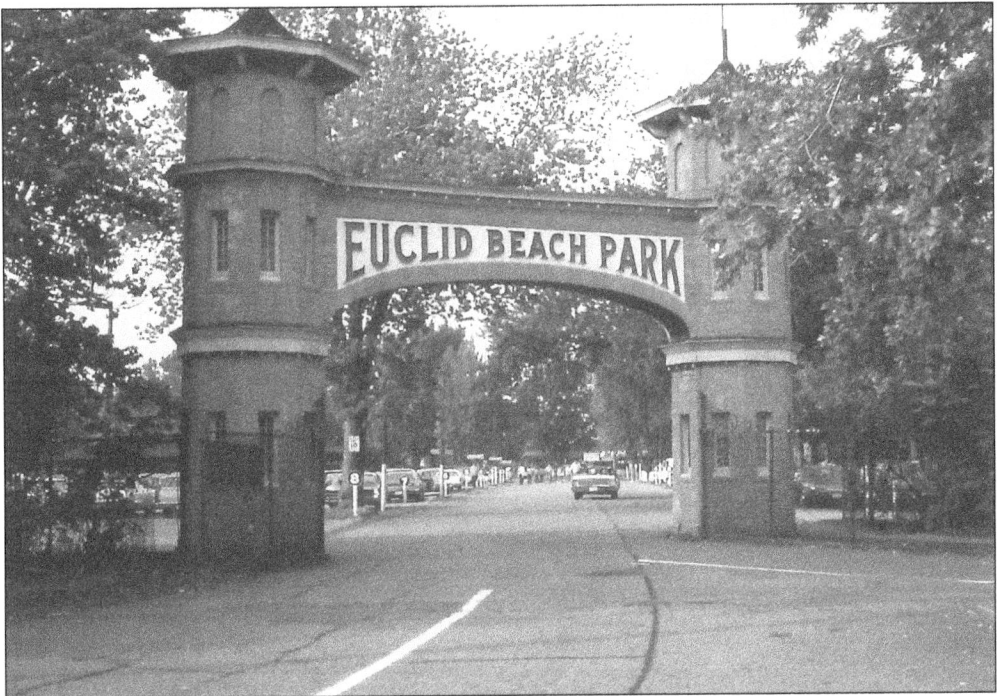

The Euclid Beach Arch, as seen in this image, was constructed in the early 1920s. It was made of wood and stood at the entrance unchanged until 1927, when it was covered in permastone.

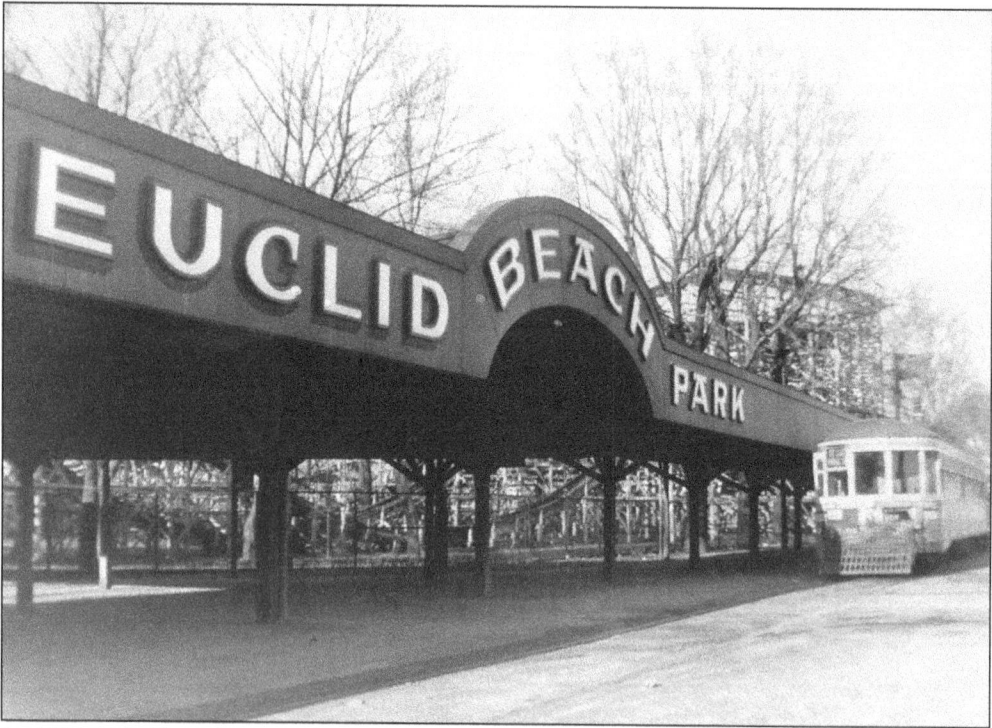

In 1904, D.S. Humphrey made an agreement with the Cleveland Traction Company to run trolleys into his park. By 1924, the streetcar station had been moved to a location near Lake Shore Boulevard. The view above shows a streetcar at the entrance to Euclid Beach. The trolleys ran on a close schedule so visitors never had a long wait for a car. The view below shows a modernized streetcar leaving the turnaround on to Lake Shore Boulevard and heading back to town.

This stand stood right across from the trolley entrance to Euclid Beach Park on the north side of Lake Shore Boulevard. Open year-round, it had all of the goodies available in the park, including sandwiches, hot dogs, pie, candy kisses, popcorn, popcorn balls, carbonated beverages, peanuts, Frozen Whip, and hot coffee. It ceased operations for several years after the park closed but later became a fruit and vegetable stand. When construction started on the new apartments, the stand was demolished.

Once the trolleys were retired, the entrance became the bus turnaround. The station wagon is in the parking lot for the Lake Shore Boulevard stand, which not only sold Humphrey products but also had a "comfort station"—a washroom available for those waiting for a ride home.

This is a view of the campground entrance in the 1960s. Today, it is a mobile-home park. During the Humphrey years, the campground had some concrete cottages, homes, and areas for tents. Presently, a few of the original structures remain but not this entrance building.

This poured concrete building at the west end of the park housed the Humphrey Office and was where park business was conducted. Here, job applications were filled out and pay envelopes distributed. The First-Aid Station and the Lost-and-Found were also located here.

More examples of Humphrey concrete construction are the cottages, which were built in 1915 in the campgrounds. They provided greater comfort to visitors than the tents, which could also be rented at the park during summer overnight stays.

Upon arriving at the Euclid Beach Park's main parking lot, visitors would first walk to the Log Cabin to register for their picnic/event badges, have their hand stamped, or pick up their park tickets. The Log Cabin was the headquarters for community, group, or company picnics, and many of those events included dancing in the Dance Pavilion before the evening was over.

Each year, the Cleveland Automobile Club would transport children from the Parmadale Orphanage to Euclid Beach. The Humphrey Company donated the park and its rides, while park employees donated their time. This event always took place on a Monday, the day the park was normally closed for maintenance. The Auto Club provided a box lunch for the children and park employees.

The Northeast Community Association held its first picnic at the Euclid Beach Park on July 24, 1957. One of the main events held was a beauty contest. A Collinwood High School graduate became the first Miss Northeast beauty queen. Many beauty contests were held at Euclid Beach over the years.

This photograph shows a piggyback race. It was simple fun at Euclid Beach at many of the company picnics: three-legged races, sack races, and candy scrambles were the order of the day. Most winners of the races were awarded a very nice prize. In the background are parts of the Thriller and Racing Coaster tracks.

Skee Ball was located in a wooden building attached to the west side of the Colonnade. Machines lined three walls with a large, common walkway in the center where a change booth was located. There were two different sized machines available for play. The mechanical games were manufactured by the National Skee Ball Company of Coney Island, New York. Skee Ball was one of only a handful of attractions that required actual change rather than tickets. These machines did not dispense tickets that could be redeemed for prizes; players merely tested their skill level.

Installed at Euclid Beach in 1938, the Flying Scooters was located in front of the Colonnade and Skee Ball. It was one of the first rides that visitors encountered when entering the park. The ride had eight cars, which were painted to resemble butterflies; each could hold one or two people. The groups pictured in both photographs were members of the Green Thumb Club, which was a horticultural program of the Cleveland Public Schools sponsored by the *Cleveland Plain Dealer*.

The Flying Scooters was a popular ride among those who wanted to fly. Riders were required to fasten a seat belt that would hold them in securely. By moving the front wing, riders could control the car's movement. With the front wing going to the left, they would streak upward. At its highest arc, the ride cars would appear to be in danger of colliding into the facade of the Colonnade building. A right turn of the wing would bring the high-flying passengers back down to earth.

The Colonnade was built in 1924 using the Humphrey's poured concrete process. It was just 400 square feet shy of being a full acre under the one roof. The original design included a second floor; however, it was never added. During the Depression, the Humphreys maintained a garden on the roof of the Colonnade. The produce was distributed amongst the year-round employees to help them through the hard times.

The Colonnade housed most of the rides in Kiddieland, including a refreshment stand, photograph booth, shooting gallery, souvenir stand, and Frozen Whip stand. It also contained many picnic tables and benches where parents kept a watchful eye on their children. Many picnickers were able to enjoy their meals even if it was raining.

Kiddieland was located in the Colonnade; many of the kiddie rides were smaller versions of adult rides in the big park. The Kiddie Ferris Wheel was located under a skylight and barely cleared the ceiling as it turned.

The Kiddie Pony Ride was always popular because children got the sensation of riding in an actual horse and buggy. It was designed so the horses would move up and down, causing the buggies to bounce.

The Fairy Whip was a small version of the Adult Dippy Whip. Children sat in a car that moved slowly along the straight portion of the oval track, and then the car whipped quickly around each curved end.

The Kiddie Carousel was a W.F. Mangels machine, which was installed at Euclid Beach in the early 1920s; it had two rows of hand-carved wooden horses and two small chariots. Parents could ride next to their small children.

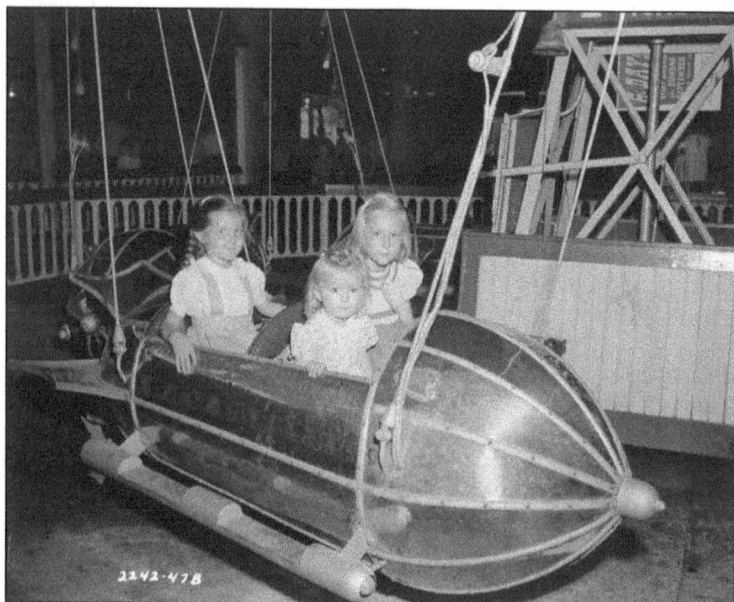

Like its adult ride counterpart, the Kiddie Rocket Ship ride cars were designed and constructed by Euclid Beach's maintenance employees to replace the original airplane-style cars. The allure of the gleaming, polished, stainless steel cars made this ride one of the most popular in Kiddieland.

The Hand Cars were located next to the Sleepy Hollow Railroad. Children were required to turn a wheel with their hands to make the cars move. It was short-lived because of the length of the ride. Many children could not make it around the track, which made it impractical on busy days. The ride operator would have to go out and bring the car and child back.

The Live Pony Ride track was leased by the Humphreys to a family from Chardon, Ohio. They brought in their ponies and carts and charged tickets issued by the park.

The Kiddie Mill Chute was a small version of Over the Falls. Kids rode in a small boat in a concrete channel and over a small hill. The pace was leisurely and it took an unusually long length of time to traverse the course. The Kiddie Turnpike can be seen in the background.

The Kiddie Hook and Ladder was one of the children's rides not within the Colonnade. Riders lined up outside next to the maintenance building. The Kiddie Hook and Ladder was a 1951 Crosley truck designed to resemble a small fire truck. Children were secured with a hinged ladder that would fold down in front of them.

The Frozen Whip was soft ice cream served in a sugar cone. The customer could watch as the frozen confection dropped into a stainless steel bowl. A long-handled spoon was used to pick up the ice cream and slide it into the cone. Frozen Whip would melt quickly so it had to be eaten fast. Most visitors will remember not only the taste and texture but also the brain freeze that resulted from eating it too quickly.

This stand was located across the Midway from the Frozen Whip stand. The popcorn and popcorn balls were made on the premises in this stand, so the purchaser always knew that the product was fresh. The candy kisses were made in a building behind this stand. The woman in the booth would collect tickets for purchases as the visitor exited.

The souvenir stand was located just under the roof of the Colonnade on the north side of the building. Park visitors could buy souvenirs, such as an ashtray, photograph album, plate, or any number of items printed with scenes of Euclid Beach. At the west end of the souvenir stand, parents could buy balloons for the kids.

A walk-through attraction, the Surprise House opened in 1935; it was originally named the FunScience Hall. Two enclosures in the front of the building housed Laughing Sal and Laughing Sam. Sal fascinated and scared patrons until the park closed. Sam was removed in the 1950s, and his enclosure was blocked off.

A "chopper" operator was located at the entrance to each of the adult rides. Surprise House patrons would place their tickets on a conveyor belt, which would carry them into the chopper, where they were shredded and collected in a cloth bag. At the end of the day, the bag was taken to the office, where the contents were weighed to determine the number of patrons who rode that day.

Laughing Sal was manufactured by the Old King Cole Company in Canton, Ohio. She was one of the estimated 300 that were produced and sold to various amusement parks by the Philadelphia Toboggan Company. Her hands, feet, and head were crafted from papier-mâché. She laughed incessantly as her torso rocked back and forth and her arms and head swung wildly. Her laugh was generated from a hidden phonograph and its stack of 78-rpm records.

The Surprise House had moving staircases and floors, tilted rooms, air holes, and a wishing well. From the front, it was possible to see people going over a small bridge with moving floors; there was also a passage with a regular floor. The elf frightened passersby with his unexpected shrill whistle.

The wishing well, which this boy is looking into, offered a view of a mermaid in early years. In the late 1930s, the Humphreys, who were always interested in new technology, installed a television monitor that showed other patrons in the Surprise House from cameras in different areas with fish swimming around them.

This was either called the "dizzy" or "tilted" room. The floor was slanted quite steeply, and the walls were perpendicular to the slanted floor, not the ground. This created an illusion that made it extremely difficult to stand upright.

Before exiting the Surprise House, visitors would pass a bank of mirrors constructed to distort their image. These girls appear to be very skinny in the mirror near the center of the picture, while the next mirror would make them appear grossly overweight. This was one of the most popular areas in the attraction.

The Bubble Bounce was installed in 1939 and remained through the end of the 1956 season. It was one of only two rides at Euclid Beach that had a garden hose at the operator's station to clean up after riders who became ill after experiencing the ride's dizzying effects.

Riders would sit in bubble-shaped cars, which could hold up to four adults. In the center of the car was a wheel that riders could pull on either side of to make the car turn in a clockwise or counter-clockwise direction. As the entire platform turned, the operator controlled an air valve that would tilt the platform at about a 10-degree angle. A good operator could lower the platform through a series of jerky bounces to heighten the ride's intensity.

The Rotor came to the park in 1957 as a replacement for the Bubble Bounce. It was a watch-and/or-ride attraction. Those who rode would enter into a very large barrel. As the barrel spun faster and faster, they would be pressed against the wall and then the floor would drop. Riders would be suspended against the wall until the operator would slow the Rotor and they would gently slide down. After the ride finished spinning, everyone moved toward the center white post while the floor went back up. Occasionally, the seams of someone's pants would split. They would be directed to the office, where the pants would be repaired by a seamstress free of charge.

The Sleepy Hollow Railroad came to Euclid Beach in 1926. It had a steam engine, but after a short time in operation the maintenance crew converted it to run on compressed air for safety reasons. While the train was in the station, the engineer would attach an air hose to the tender behind the engine. The train was loaded and ready to leave by the time the tank was filled with enough air for one trip around the course.

In 1948, the old train was replaced with a modern, diesel-style locomotive and sleek, new passenger cars. The *Euclid Beach Chief*, however, was fueled with gasoline not diesel. The new train traveled in a counter-clockwise direction to ease passenger loading and unloading.

The train wove its way under and around the structure of the Racing Coaster and passed by the miniature village of Sleepy Hollow, which was made up of buildings such as city hall, a church, a school, and houses. There were streetlights, so at night the town was lit up. The train passed through a tunnel and over a goldfish pond on its way back to the station. The Sleepy Hollow sign was created at the park using cement as the material. The back wall of the Surprise House is seen to the left in the photograph below.

Over the Falls was constructed in 1931 as the Mill Chute by the Philadelphia Toboggan Company. When the Scenic Railway was removed in 1937, the channel was extended, more curves added, the hill was raised from 30 to 37 feet, and the angle was increased from 20 to 50 degrees. This resulted in a dramatic increase of speed.

A boat is about to enter the tunnel while a curtain of water drops across the opening. Just as the boat was about to be covered with water, a trip lever under the boat shut it off. After passing under the curtain, the lever was released, and the water was turned back on. All of the scenes in the dark tunnel were painted with luminous paint, and the water was chemically treated so that it gave off an eerie glow under the blacklights.

Riders are poised at the brink of doom. As the boat reached the top of the hill, it seemed to hang for a while and teeter, increasing the anticipation for the plunge to the lake below.

As the boat plunged down the hill, it would make a whooshing sound that added to the anticipation of being splashed when the boat hit the lake. The end is near, as the riders and boat are about to enter the dock with a splash.

63

The boats on Over the Falls floated through the channel—there were no chains or belts to move them. The water was moved around the channel by the large waterwheel at the base of the hill. The wheel would lift the water from the back of the hill and move it to the lake.

A tranquil winter scene at Euclid Beach, this photograph shows Sleepy Hollow in the foreground, the Over the Falls hill in the background, and the Racing Coaster hill beyond. All are covered with a dusting of snow.

This is the entrance of the Racing Coaster with its Art Deco facade; the letters were mounted about a foot away from the background and were lit from behind at night. This ride was designed and built by John Miller in 1913 and featured three-car trains with three seats in each car. Riders rode with competition between the two trains. The trains were either red or green; often, riders picked their favorite color.

This photograph shows the train leaving from the right side of the loading platform. The train would circle around and under the exit platform before starting up the lift hill. Of all the coasters at Euclid Beach, only the Racing Coaster and the Aero Dips had locking lap bars.

Two views of the down side of the lift hill are seen here. The ride operator could control the speed of the chain that pulled the trains up the hill. If there was a pretty girl on the ride, that train would most likely win with the help of the ride operator.

This is a view of most of the Racing Coaster's tracks. The tops of the Thriller and the Flying Turns are visible to the right in the photograph. In the center is the village of Sleepy Hollow, with the train tracks winding under the roller coaster.

This photograph shows the Racing Coaster lift hill and part of the Thriller's lift hill. The tallest point on the Racing Coaster was 60.6 feet, approximately 10 feet shorter than that of the Thriller.

The red and green trains are in a near dead heat as they race back to the unloading station. The outcome will not be known until the trains enter the tunnel at the end of the home stretch.

Two trains are coming to a stop at the unloading platform. The coaster track was laid out on a continuous circuit and puzzled many riders where and when it switched over. The operator on the left has his foot raised, ready to step on the running board and ride the train to the final brake, where he will direct riders to exit on the center platform.

The Thriller was constructed at Euclid Beach Park in 1924 by the Philadelphia Toboggan Company. This mid-1920s photograph shows the view from the lift hill with a train seen entering the unloading platform. The construction cost in 1923 was $90,000; it was said to have paid for itself in the first season. This shows the building before the Art Deco facade was installed.

The Thriller was always a very popular ride at Euclid Beach. In the early days, it was not unusual to see three trains running to accommodate the crowds; however, by the 1950s, no more than two trains were ever run at one time due to safety reasons.

The train is at the unloading station of the platform. The brakeman to the left is about to release the brake and allow the train to roll down to the loading station. The lap restraints are welded tubing; it lacked a locking mechanism like those found on most other coasters.

This train is going west over the bus entrance on its way toward the parking lot, where it would make a hairpin turn to begin its last leg to return back to the loading station.

The train is moving north over the "bunny hop" hills toward the unloading station. The Thriller cars have three different sets of wheels: one set rode on the top of the track, one rode against the inside of the track to maintain direction, and another rode under the track to keep the train from lifting off the track.

The lift hill on the Thriller was 71 feet, five inches tall. The original second hill was 60 feet, six inches but was lowered because the trains lost too much speed. The clacking sound was the noise made by the safety dogs as the train went up the lift hill, which prevented the train from rolling backwards in the event of a power failure.

Excited riders are heading into the unloading station. The total length of the track was 2,927 feet. It averaged 40 miles per hour and had a capacity of 800 people per hour. Herb Schmeck designed this out-and-back coaster.

This is a view of the east end of the Midway showing the Art Deco–style facades of the Thriller and the Flying Turns, which were in place from the early 1930s through the remaining years of the park's life.

The Flying Turns, designed by John Miller and J.N. Bartlett, was constructed during the summer season in 1930. Each of the three train cars rode in a wooden barrel that resembled a bobsled course.

The super structure of the Flying Turns was constructed of a metal framework and cypress wood slats to create a barrel. The 1.5-inch-thick cypress panels required constant attention from the maintenance staff.

The train cars were designed to look like small aircraft and fit two people. The cars rode on six rubber casters, which swiveled 360 degrees. The train was pulled up the lift hill by a chain, and once it reached the top of the hill it was freewheeling; gravity and centrifugal force were in control.

The Flying Turns was the last of the high rides built by the Humphreys at Euclid Beach Park. The black marks in the barrel show where the rubber wheels came in contact with the surface of the barrel. A band of gray paint indicates where the ride cars would travel. Any park employees working in the barrel would know where to stand outside of the painted area to be safe. It was popular with young couples and considered a "date ride."

This view gives an idea of the speed of the ride relative to the barrel. In reality, the average speed of the train on the Flying Turns was 25 miles per hour, but most riders felt they were going much faster.

This train has just come in to the unloading area. Nighttime was a great time to ride since riders could not see what was coming next once they rode below the upper level. The Flying Turns, unlike the other Euclid Beach roller coasters, had only its lift hill and upper level lit at night.

The Rock-O-Plane was located at the east end of the Midway between the Flying Turns and the Laff in the Dark. Similar to a Ferris wheel, there were eight cars, which were really wire cages. The riders sat on a bench and the cage door was closed and locked. In front of the riders was a steel ring welded on a bar. By pulling back on the ring, the rider could lock the cage on its axis, so when the ride turned, the cage would turn the rider upside down.

The Ferris Wheel was installed at the park in 1963 where the Great American Racing Derby once stood. It was built by the Eli Bridge Company of Jacksonville, Illinois. This was the second and final Ferris Wheel installed on the park grounds.

The Scrambler, a mid-1960s addition that replaced the Rock-O-Planes, was located near the trailer park. It was designed and built by the Eli Bridge Company, which described it as the ultimate double-rotation ride. The entire ride mechanism spun around a control axis, and three pods of four cars each spun around their own central axis. The lighter person was always encouraged by the ride operator to go into the car first since the motion of the ride at full speed would push he or she into the person riding on the outside part of the seat.

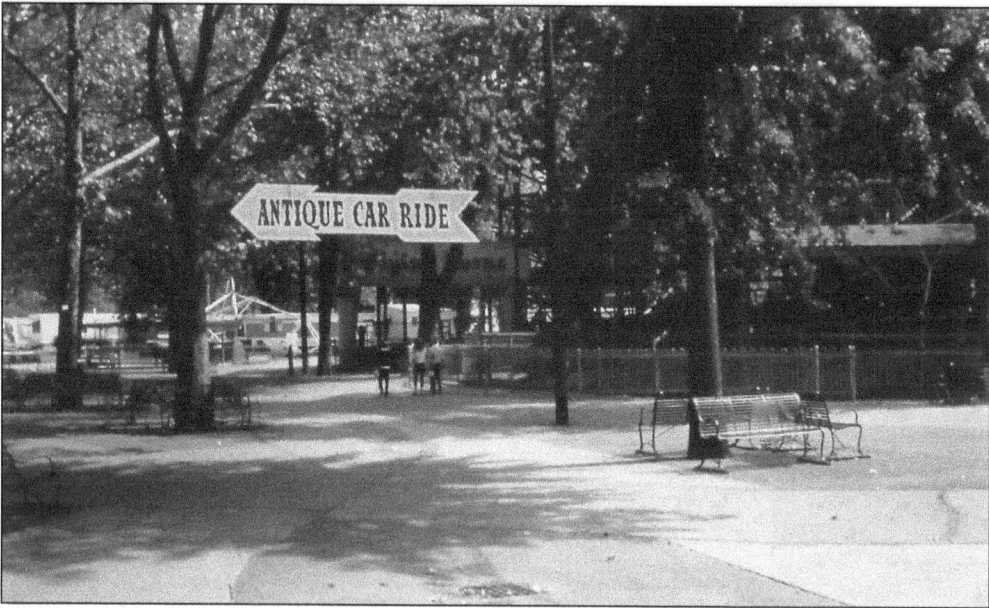

A sign was located on the Midway in front of the Racing Coaster directing potential riders to the Antique Cars. In the background, the Scrambler and the mobile homes in the trailer park are visible. Three of the comfortable steel park benches that provided much needed relaxation for park patrons can be seen in the foreground.

In later years, the Skating Rink was leased to the Cavaliers, who were a private skating club. After the rink failed to draw sufficient skaters in the 1961 and 1962 seasons, the Humphreys decided to install the Antique Cars in the underused building.

The track, with a center rail, was laid out around and about the Skating Rink. It had the look of an early-1900s farm area with a barn front, farm animals scattered around, and replica gaslights. The Gavioli Band Organ provided music just as it had for the skaters since 1910.

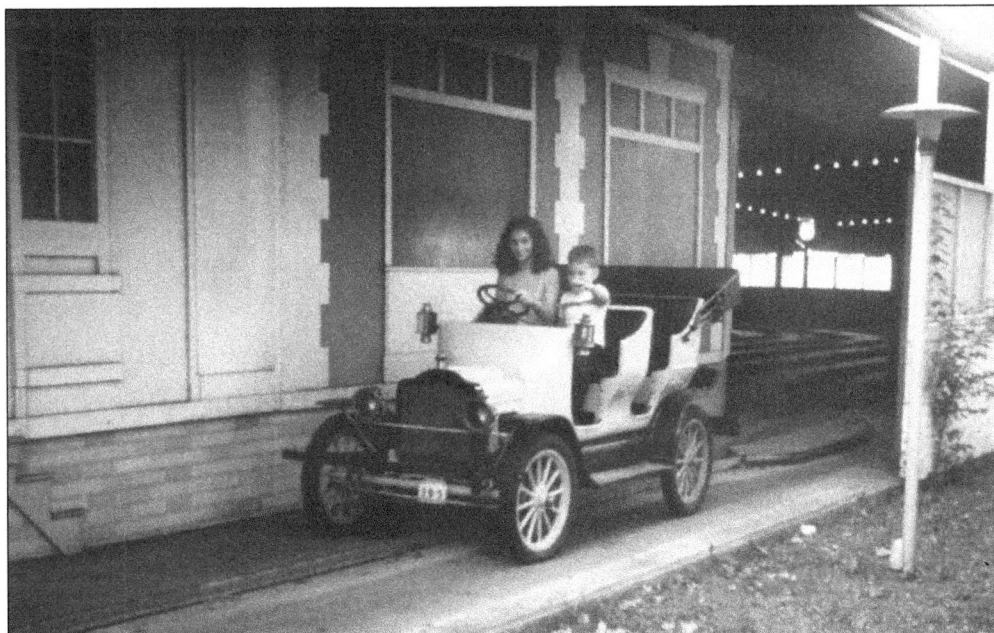

One of the Antique Cars is shown leaving the indoor portion of the ride heading to the unloading areas. Riders would travel in front of a turn-of-the-century building facade before disembarking and heading to their next park adventure.

When the Dodgem was originally installed in 1921, the cars were designed to move in exactly the opposite direction from which the driver intended. If for example, the driver steered to the left, the car would go right. The cars pictured here were front-wheel-drive replacements purchased from the Dodgem Corporation of Lawrence, Massachusetts, in the 1930s. The building was 143 feet by 90 feet and reportedly the largest Dodgem track in the United States. Those who rode at Euclid Beach might remember the ride operator instructing everyone, "Traffic moves one way and one way only. No head-on bumping."

Euclid Beach's Laff in the Dark had many stunts, such as an owl flying overhead and a collision with a train. The ride was completely dark inside with lights used only to illuminate the gags and stunts. The sign sported the Art Deco look that most of the rides had from the 1930s on. One of the Euclid Beach Police officers stands in the foreground of the photograph. From the early days, Euclid Beach had its own police force.

The ride operator would not release the car into the attraction until a green light appeared on his or her control panel. This light indicated that the previous car was safely ahead so that the illusions would be timed properly. A sign above the entrance advised riders to keep their arms inside the car.

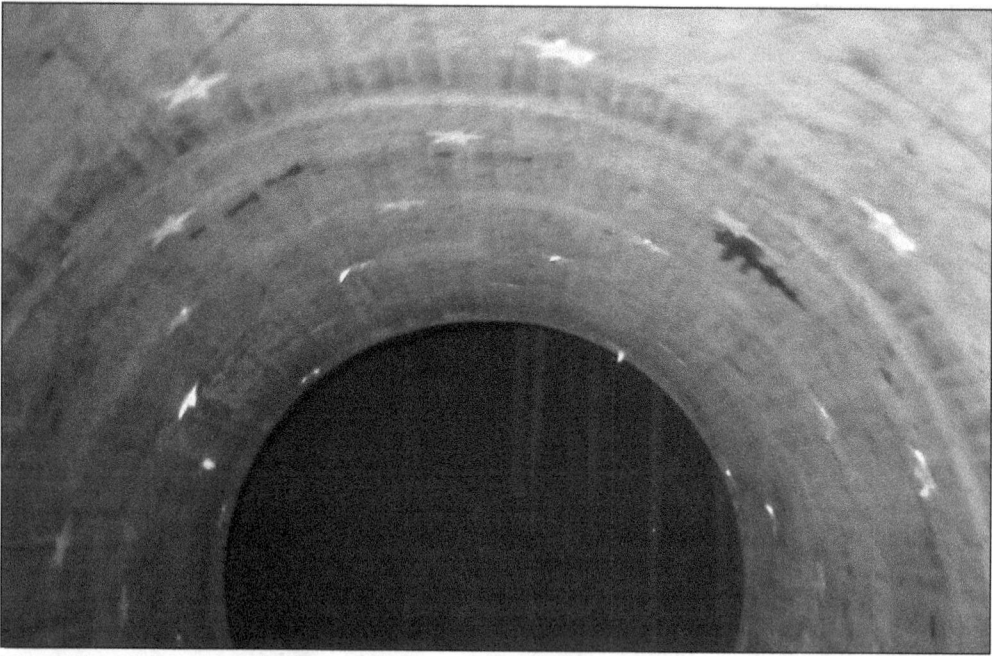

The Laff in the Dark was built in 1931. Though it contained many stunts, such as the caged lion, the one that most park visitors remember was the Barrel of Stars. The large barrel was built to revolve around the track. It was decided to decorate the spiral with luminous stars and darken the area when the car went through. Upon completing the mechanism for the barrel, workers stood on the track to watch it turn. With the lights turned off, the workers began to feel as though they were falling over. They had hit on a splendid illusion without even trying. It was one of the last stunts that riders passed through before the exit.

The Humphrey mansion was located in the far northeast corner of the campgrounds. When it was originally built, it was called the Castle Inn; it served as a hotel where people could stay and eat home-cooked meals. Dudley Sherman Humphrey II converted it into a residence for himself and his family. He died in his bedroom at the residence on September 7, 1933.

David Humphrey Scott, founder of Euclid Beach Park Now, grew up in this house. Scott's mother was a member of the Humphrey family. The house was located in the west end of the park. His father was the chief park engineer from the early 1900s until his death in the 1930s. Scott often said that when the park closed and people went home, it became his playground.

The Velvet Coaster, renamed Aero Dips in the 1920s, was built in 1909. The ride was designed and built by John Miller, who constructed the Derby Racer in 1913. This photograph shows the lift hill and the turn over the loading platform. The small building to the left of the lift hill is the garage for the Auto Train.

On August 20, 1964, this group visited Euclid Beach as part of an outing organized by the *Cleveland Plain Dealer*. The train is leaving the loading platform and will soon be pulled up the lift hill. The cars on the Aero Dips and the Racing Coaster were interchangeable.

This photograph shows the turn over the loading platform. The building straight ahead was the Dance Pavilion. The tower to the right was the Rocket Ship ride.

The people seen here on the Aero Dips train were part of a family reunion held at Euclid Beach Park. As with the Racing Coaster, a locking lap bar held riders in their seats securely.

When visitors approached the Penny Arcade, they were greeted with many sounds of machines being played, people laughing, and flashing lights. Some machines dispensed pictures of popular actors and actresses, while others tested skill or strength. The most popular machine was a mechanical Grandma, which would dispense fortunes in a rolled-up piece of paper for a penny.

Although new amusements were added to the Penny Arcade over the years, many of the old staples remained. For the cost of a penny, these hand-cranked movie viewers featured a number of titles, ranging from sports and Westerns to comedy. The Penny Arcade was one of a handful of attractions not owned by the Humphreys but leased to private operators.

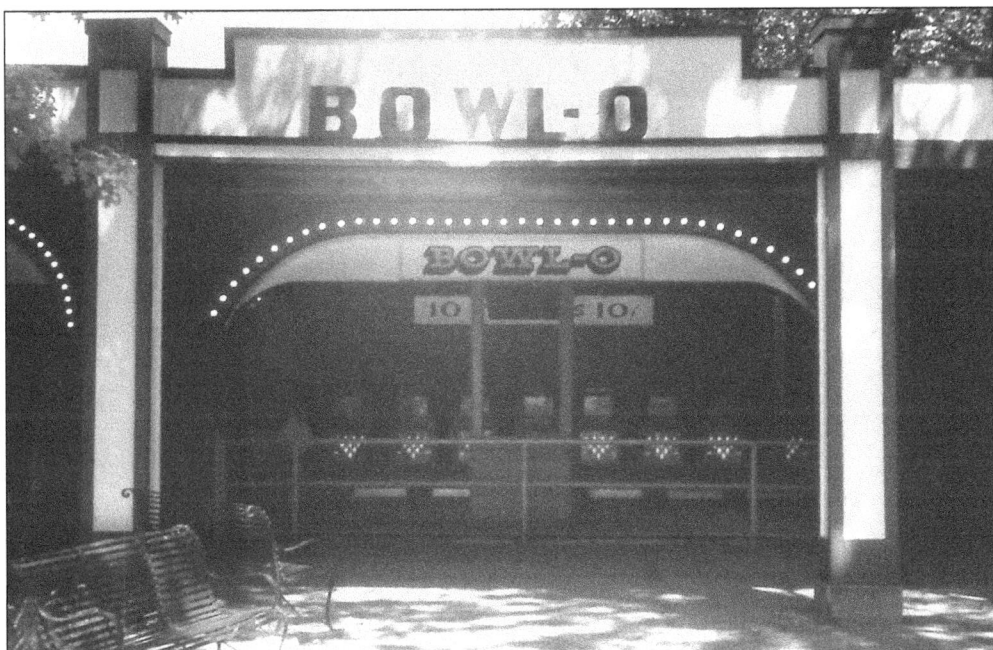

The Bowl-O machines were located next to the Penny Arcade. The six bowling machines had a hanging rack of pins and an electronic scoreboard. For a dime, anyone could test their skills and try to outscore their friends.

The Commando Guns were located next to the Bowl-O concession. There were five pneumatically fired BB guns. The goal was to shoot moving and stationary bull's-eye targets. The ever-resourceful Humphreys designed the booth with a sloping floor so that the used BBs returned to the guns to be used again.

In this photograph of faded glory, the Victorian-era Dance Pavilion shows wear and tear in the last days of the park's operation. The building was one of the few spanning the entire life of the park from 1895 to 1969.

This grand dance floor of 18,000 square feet, made of red maple, could accommodate 1,000 couples at one time. The lighting and fixtures date this photograph to 1927 or earlier.

VIC STUART

Vic Stuart was the last house bandleader at the Dance Pavilion. His band was in residence from 1945 to 1959. Some other well-known bands that played at Euclid Beach were Lawrence Welk and Benny Goodman, as well as Tommy and Jimmy Dorsey. In the 1950s and 1960s, polka bands also played in the Dance Pavilion. The Larry Revell Orchestra is pictured below. They appeared at the Dance Pavilion in the 1930s right after an interior remodeling that featured the relocation of the bandstand.

The Giant Slide, located near the Dance Pavilion, was added in 1962. Riders would climb the stairway to the top and be given a burlap sack for their journey down the spiral-shaped slide.

The Swingin' Gyms was comprised of separate steel cages that pivoted. By shoving back and forth, riders attempted to get the cages to spin 360 degrees.

In 1921, the Great American Racing Derby was constructed at Euclid Beach Park on the Midway next to the Carousel. It was a product of the Prior and Church Company of Venice, California. The area in front of this 114-foot-wide building also served as a loading and unloading station for the Auto Train.

The Great American Racing Derby was a unique merry-go-round. It had 64 hand-carved wooden horses, four abreast, designed to hold up to two riders. The horses moved forward and backwards, as well as up and down.

In the early years, when the bell rang indicating the end of the ride, the horse in the lead would receive an American flag, which was placed in a small hole on the left side of the horse's head by the ride operator. The lucky winner received a free ride. Riders could watch the operators jump on and off the platform as it was moving (while facing the horses); their animated dance was nicknamed the "Derby Shuffle."

Even though home scales were familiar fixtures in American homes by the early 1950s, the penny scales located at various spots throughout the park were always popular. This particular scale was between the Surprise House and a concession stand that sold popcorn balls, candy kisses, and peanuts. The man pictured here was visiting as part of a Goodyear Tire and Rubber Company picnic in 1940.

During the 1930s, the Carousel's overall appearance was changed to reflect the Art Deco movement. The mechanism and the horses were painted mostly white, and the spelling of "carousel" was altered to the double "r" as seen in the sign pictured here.

Before the ride started, a bell would ring. As people rode, the North Tonawanda band organ would play. When the bell rang again, they knew the ride on the Grand Carousel was over, and it was time to head for another ride.

The Euclid Beach Grand Carousel was manufactured by the Philadelphia Toboggan Company for the 1910 season. It was a large, four-row machine with 58 hand-carved horses and two chariots. The stationary outside row horses were nearly life-size. The horse on the outer row, pictured here, has been nicknamed "Stars and Stripes," "Flag Horse," and "Old Glory."

The Carousel's outer row had two hand-carved wooden chariots. When PTC No. 19 was delivered, the woman and cherubs that embellished the outside were nude. Upon seeing this, the Humphreys insisted the figures be covered up. Artisans from the Philadelphia Toboggan Company created draping to cover the exposed areas.

96

This photograph shows the intricate artwork added to the upper scenery panels during the 1930s, when the Carousel received its Art Deco makeover. This 1964 photograph shows a girl who took part in a company-sponsored outing.

This is a rare view of the North Tonawanda band organ facade and the smaller, inner row of jumper horses on the Carousel. The Carousel's band organ was one of three that played at Euclid Beach; the others being the Artizan Band Organ at the Rocket Ships and the Gavioli in the Skating Rink.

The Fountain was centered within the circular pool, located on the beach next to the Pier. Swimming in the pool was reserved for the guests of the cottages, campgrounds, and employees of the park. In the evening, colored lights, which had been installed under each ring, were turned on to create a dazzling sight.

At the request of the Humphreys, the Euclid Beach maintenance department began designing replacements for the Aeroplanes that would emulate the rockets in the popular Buck Rogers movie serials. The polished stainless steel ride cars were built at the park and installed by park employees. All four sides of the tower were designed with five rings, with a star in each that was lit at night. The track for the Bug is visible in the foreground.

At full speed, Rocket Ships skim the trees that lined the promenade above the beach. A configuration of bars slid across the openings to keep riders in their seats, and landing lights were located on the front of each of the pontoons on both sides of the ship. According to a Cleveland urban legend, one of the Rocket Ships broke loose from the tower and landed in the lake—this never occurred. Engineers determined that it would be impossible for all eight cables to break at one time.

Riders head down the exit ramp before the next group is allowed on the platform to board the car of their choice. At rest, the Rocket Ships sat snugly against the loading platform so riders could enter and exit safely. As they exited, patrons passed an opening in the wall, which gave them a glimpse of how the center shaft was driven and the brake system operated.

Though Euclid Beach was a place of fun and excitement during the day, when the sun set over Lake Erie and the lights came on throughout the park, it became a land of enchantment. Visitors could enjoy the same rides they rode in daylight, but at night it was a different experience. The lights played a large part in the way that the park closed each night. The park manager would ride his bike from the office to the Thriller about 15 minutes before closing. The lights on top of the Thriller lift hill could be seen from most of the park. A few minutes before closing each ride, someone stood at each electric breaker box. When the manager gave his signal, the Thriller went dark, and within 5 to 10 seconds all the rides were dark.

The Bug was installed at the park in 1928 and was designed and built by the Traver Engineering Company. The popular ride paid for itself by the beginning of July in its first year of operation. It operated until closing day and was subsequently dismantled. The cars were sold to Geauga Lake Park in Aurora, Ohio, and were used for parts.

There were two ways of bringing the Bug in to the platform. On a regular day, there was a position on the track where the motors could be turned off, and it would coast in after two and a half turns. On busy days, the operator would stop the ride by reversing the motors, and it would stop in only one and a half revolutions.

Pictured here is one of the two large drinking fountains, which were located on either side of the Dance Pavilion. They were a welcome sight to park patrons on the warm and sultry days of summer.

In the area in front of the Coffee Break and the Bug, there was a sign that read, "Look for Lost Children Here." There was a bench where lost children could comfortably wait for their parents.

In 1966, the Coffee Break replaced the Dippy Whip in the old Avenue Theatre building. The ride cars were designed to resemble coffee cups and saucers. As the cups traveled through their circular journey, the ride was designed to give passengers the illusion that the cars might actually collide into one another.

The Turnpike cars were brought to Euclid Beach in 1962 and were located west of the Bug and the Rocket Ships. The cars were made by the Arrow Manufacturing Company. They were powered by an eight-horsepower gasoline engine and kept on course by a steel center rail.

To further enhance the driving experience, the Humphreys constructed a replica of a Standard Oil station in the center of a track section. During the 1960s, these stations were a familiar sight on almost any northeast Ohio street corner.

The bridge is part of the figure-eight-configured Turnpike course. The bridge structure remains to this day as a walkway on the driveway to the apartment building entrance. In the background, through the trees, the tower of the Rocket Ship ride is visible.

Cars are lined up and ready for additional passengers. Ride operators could hop onto a small step on the side of the car and push a handle to bring the cars to a safe stop when entering the unloading area. After the park closed, the cars were again used at Shady Lake Park and then moved to Old Indiana Family Fun Park, where they were sold at auction when that park closed.

106

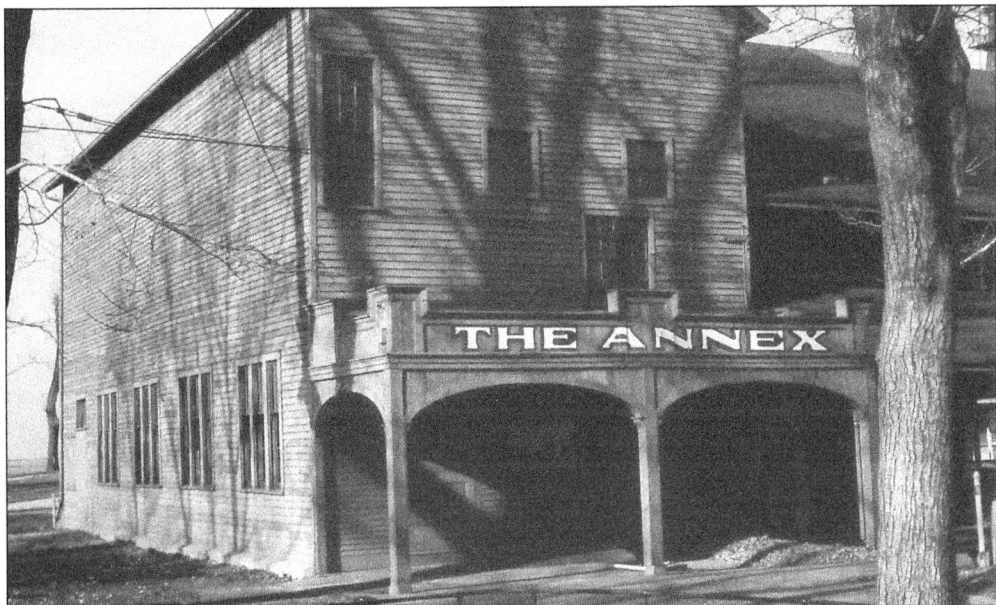

Originally, the Annex was a part of the Avenue Theatre; it was used for dressing rooms and a staging area for costumes. When the Avenue Theatre closed in 1938, the Annex became a headquarters for small picnics. It was also used as a meeting hall when park employees held their union meetings.

The ballerina on the horse served as a backdrop over the stage of the Avenue Theatre. In 1938, after the theater closed, it became the new home of the Dippy Whip. The painting remained as part of the Whip, and in the 1960s it could still be seen as part of the Coffee Break ride.

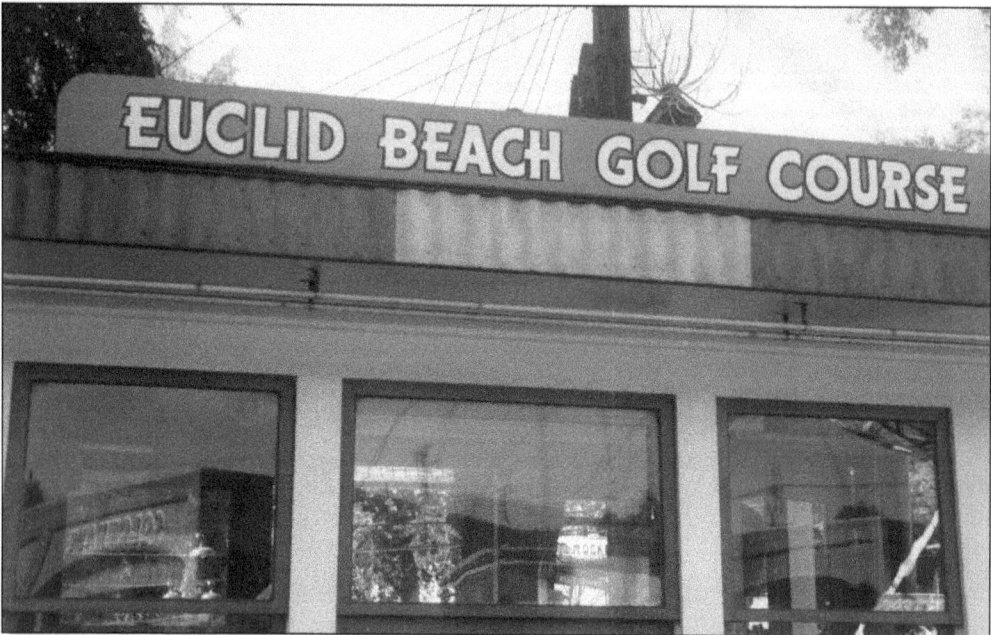

The Pee Wee Miniature Golf was built in 1950 and designed by Howard Stoneback. The golf office is where players paid with tickets to receive their clubs, balls, and scorecards. The first hole was next to the office. Players then went over a footbridge, where they played 12 more holes, and then crossed over the bridge and played the last five.

There were many obstacles at the golf course, including banked curves, hills, and dips. The 10th hole required one to putt the ball under the lighthouse. The 18th hole collected the ball to end the game.

The Maintenance Building was constructed in 1910 under the supervision of Jack Lambe, D.S. Humphrey's son-in-law. The building housed the maintenance department, warehouse, machine shop, auto mechanic, and general labor.

Each fall, a thick layer of heavy grease was applied to the surface of all the coaster tracks to protect them from the Lake Erie winter. Each spring, the maintenance crew would use long-handled scrapers and kerosene to remove the grease. This involved scraping more than 8,000 feet of roller-coaster track.

Two maintenance men replace the steel tracks on the Racing Coaster. Long carpenter clamps were used to maintain the correct gauge of the track. During World War II, when steel was in short supply, the Humphreys realized that the track at the top of the hills had less wear than at the bottom, so they had their maintenance crews swap them to extend the life of the steel.

Maintenance workers repair the track of the Bug. The Dippy Whip building (originally the Avenue Theatre) is visible in the background.

These two scenes would be familiar to anyone who traveled to Euclid Beach in an automobile. The "This Way Out" arrow sign pointed park patrons to the exit at the corner of East 156th Street and Lake Shore Boulevard. The building in the background of the photograph below is the Log Cabin.

This aerial view looking north shows Lake Shore Boulevard and the streetcar/bus entrance. On the right side is the softball field. To the left are the tracks for the Flying Turns, Thriller, Racing Coaster, and the Scenic Railway. The large building in the center is the Colonnade, which housed enough picnic tables to shelter over 1,000 people as well as a refreshment stand for food and beverages. The rectangular roof on the left is that of the Log Cabin. The extensive canopy of trees provided welcome relief on sunny days.

This aerial view of the park faces south. The bottom of the photograph shows the Pier, Fountain, Bath House, and restaurant. Just above are the Aero Dips and the open-sided Main Lunch Building, part of which was used as the Aero Dips loading platform. The Skating Rink building has a long, white skylight; just to the right of it is the Penny Arcade building. The building straight up from the Pier is the Dance Pavilion.

Three

THE MEMORIES LIVE ON

On September 28, 1969, Euclid Beach Park closed; shortly thereafter, the property was sold to developers. This photograph of the Arch was taken before the construction of the high-rise senior apartments and Manor Care nursing home on the western half of the original park property. The Arch remains to this day a gateway to yesterday's memories.

The Art Deco interior of the Dance Pavilion is pictured shortly after the park closed. It would become the victim of arson and, finally, the wrecking ball.

A lone Dodgem car, missing many of its parts, sits abandoned outside of the Skating Rink/Antique Car building. The area where the rink once stood was donated by the developers to create a public park. Today, Euclid Beach State Park remains on part of the original grounds.

The Bug track was already being disassembled in this view of the Rocket Ships. The three ships were saved from being destroyed, have been motorized, and are familiar sites at festivals and events around Greater Cleveland.

The Over the Falls structure is shown in the early stages of being demolished; in the background is the Lake Shore Boulevard run of the Thriller, awaiting its demise. The high rides were the last structures removed to clear the path for new construction.

With the reality of the park's closing, efforts were made to save pieces of the park, and many memories were saved. Here, men are removing the letters from the Flying Turns facade. Although the ride was demolished, some of the ride cars and signage were saved.

The Thriller cars are being salvaged in this photograph. Two men are directing the crane operator. One of the Thriller coaster cars has been married with the park's 1951 maintenance truck and has joined its sister ride, the Rocket Ships, on the streets of Cleveland.

The Rotor facade is pictured here. There are no more riders to watch, held captive along the walls of the "human centrifuge." Although the facade was destined for demolition, the Humphreys reinstalled the ride itself at Shady Lake.

From the beginning, the Pier required an enormous amount of maintenance and care. With the park's closure and the Humphreys' departure, Mother Nature reclaimed the Pier and the Fountain. The wooden stubs sticking out of the lake are all that remain of the Pier's pilings.

The Great American Racing Derby was sold and moved to Cedar Point in 1967. The building constructed to house the ride was exactly the same as the one at Euclid beach Park. The reasons for its early removal, only two years prior to the park's closure, were that it was sold in an effort to raise operating capital and also that it was a victim of its high maintenance.

The restored Racing Derby horses are pictured at their new home at Cedar Point. It was renamed Cedar Downs and still operates there today. The Euclid Beach Park Midway is no longer visible in the background.

Shady Lake was opened in Streetsboro, Ohio, in 1978 by the Humphrey family. Almost all of the Euclid Beach Kiddieland rides were installed at the new park except for the Kiddie Over the Falls and the Kiddie Hook and Ladder. Other rides that were familiar to beach patrons included the Turnpike, Dodgem, and Rotor. A notable new addition was the Wild Mouse ride. An entrance Arch, reminiscent of the one that greeted patrons to Euclid Beach, was constructed at the new park's Streetsboro entrance. Because the park was so far from the original Lake Shore Boulevard location, it was unable to draw large numbers of loyal customers from the past; it closed in 1982. The Arch remained until 2004, when an apartment complex was built on the site.

Euclid Beach Park Nuts (renamed Euclid Beach Park Now) held annual memorabilia shows at Euclid Square Mall in Euclid. The shows drew huge crowds eager to relive their memories of the park. Elaborate displays were constructed, including this replica of the Arch entranceway.

The iconic symbol of Euclid Beach Park, Laughing Sal was on display at many of the mall shows. Clevelanders' fascination with her continues to this day. Sal is currently part of the memorabilia collection of the Euclid Beach Boys.

The Humphreys established their farm in Wakeman, Ohio, in the 1830s. They lost it to bankruptcy at a sheriff's auction in 1890. The farm was repurchased by the Humphrey Family in 1927, and the hybrid corn used for their popcorn balls is still grown there today.

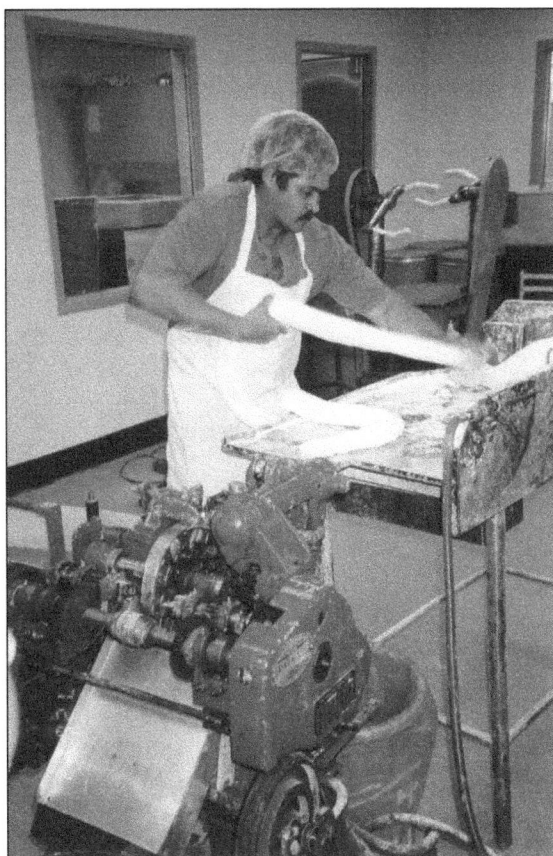

The Humphrey Popcorn Factory is located in Warrensville Heights, Ohio. The employee pictured here is using one of the original machines from the park that stretched, cut, and wrapped the candy kisses. Today, popcorn balls and kisses are familiar sights in area grocery stores and are available internationally via the Internet.

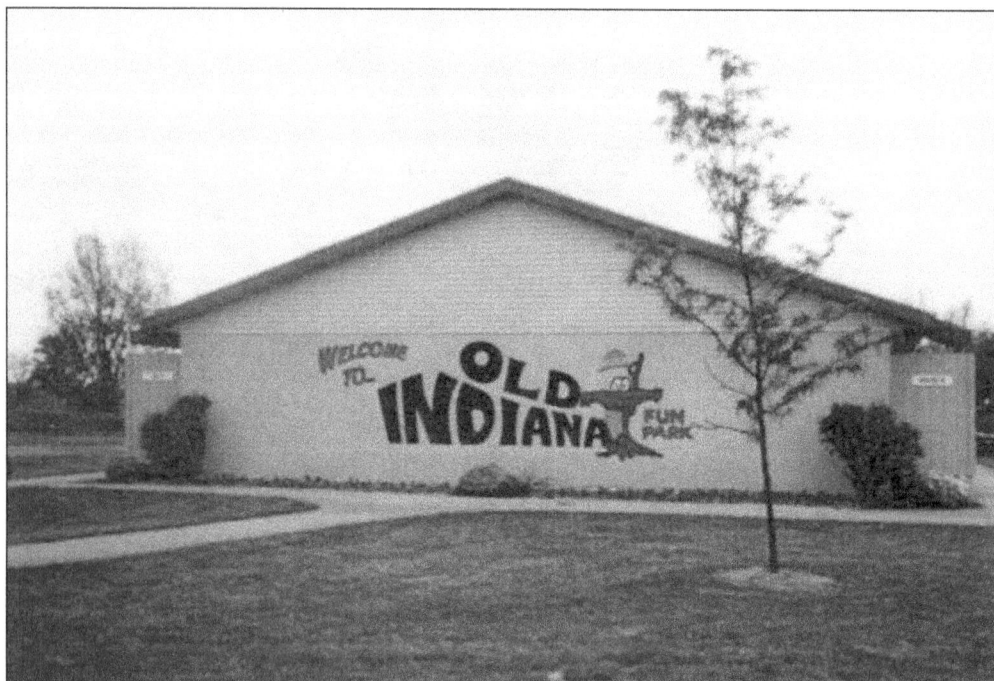

When the decision was made to close Shady Lake, all of the rides were sold to an amusement park northwest of Indianapolis, Indiana. Old Indiana Fun Park opened in 1983 and closed abruptly in 1996 after a fatal accident involving the derailment of the locomotive from the Sleepy Hollow Railroad; the *Euclid Beach Chief* derailed and overturned as it approached a curve. An auction was held on February 22, 1997, for the park's rides and fixtures.

The Euclid Beach entrance Arch was designated as a historic Cleveland landmark in 1973. In early spring 2007, a resident of the apartments located behind the entranceway collided with the east Arch tower, causing a significant amount of damage.

The Arch was repaired and rededicated in June 2007. The Rocket Ship car and the Thriller car are shown driving under the Arch, celebrating its reopening after the repair. Cleveland dignitaries present included Cleveland mayor Frank Jackson, state representative Kenny Yuko, and Ward 11 councilman Michael Polensek.

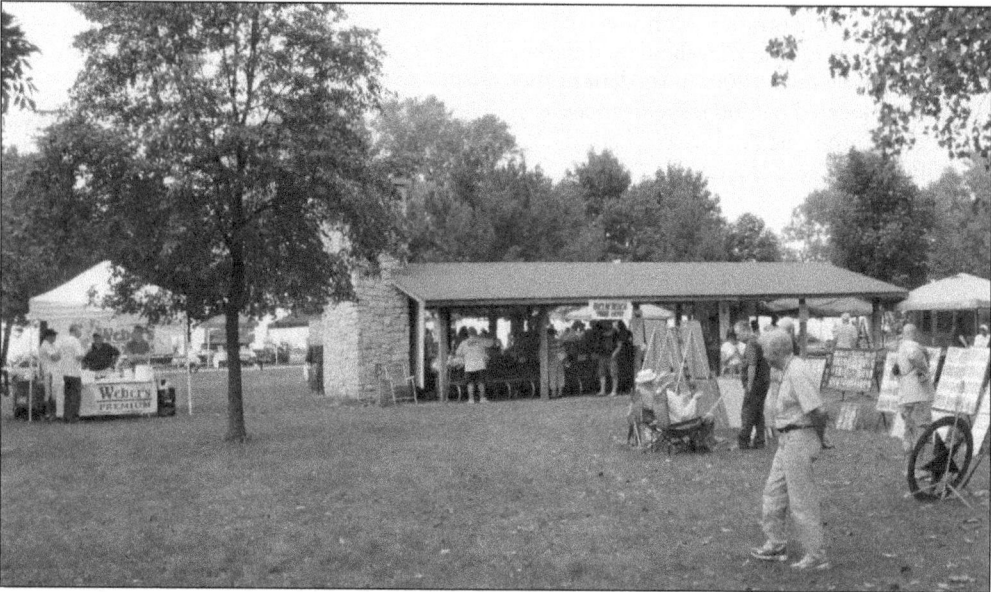

Euclid Beach Park Now, in partnership with the Ohio Department of Natural Resources and the Euclid Beach Boys, holds an annual event at the former site of the park, Remembering the Sights and Sounds of Euclid Beach Park. This annual event is held toward the end of September and roughly coincides with the park's closing date of September 28. Memorabilia is placed at the various locations where the rides once stood, and walking tours are conducted that explain the park's rich history. Souvenirs are available for sale, and a car show is held that focuses on vehicles that could have been driven to Euclid Beach (makes and models from 1895 to 1969). Attendees can still experience two of the park's signature rides by taking a short tour through the park and the adjacent apartment complex on either the Euclid Beach Boys Rocket Ship Car or Thriller Car.

Euclid Beach's Grand Carousel (PTC No. 19) was sold to Palace Playland in Old Orchard Beach, Maine, after the park closed. It operated as part of this seaside resort until 1997, when the operator decided to sell the machine due to financial difficulties.

PTC No. 19's appearance changed drastically when it operated at Old Orchard Beach. From the 1930s on at Euclid Beach Park, all the horses were painted white except for their decorative trappings. At Palace Playland, the horses were painted in pastel colors; the vaulted ceiling was removed; the decorative look of the center surround, upper and lower scenery panels, and rounding boards was changed; and the North Tonawanda Band Organ no longer played within the center surround.

In 1997, Norton Auctioneers brought the Carousel back to Cleveland, where they believed the best prices could be obtained at auction. The auction was held at Trolleyville USA in Olmstead Falls, Ohio, in conjunction with a Euclid Beach memorabilia show organized by the Euclid Beach Park Nuts.

The auction started with the sale of PTC No. 19's intricately carved Armor Horse. After all of the horses were sold individually, the auctioneer totaled all the sales figures and came up with a starting point for the entire machine. The machine sold as a whole unit for $715,000—a record price for a Carousel at that time.

After the auction, the horses were all restored, and the mechanism was placed in storage. Two sites on Cleveland's lakefront were proposed for its reinstallation, but neither plan came to fruition. In 2010, a partnership was developed between the Western Reserve Historical Society, Euclid Beach Park Now, and Cleveland's Euclid Beach Park Carousel Society. The plan is to construct a carousel pavilion as an addition to the Western Reserve Society's History Center in Cleveland's University Circle and place the carousel in operation there by the fall of 2014. The temporary display of the restored horses at Western Reserve Historical Society is pictured above, along with an architectural rendering of the carousel pavilion below.

Visit us at
arcadiapublishing.com

www.ingramcontent.com/pod-product-compliance
Lightning Source LLC
Chambersburg PA
CBHW080628110426
42813CB00006B/1634